FARMS

Vegetable Farms

Ann Thomas

MACMILLAN

Acknowledgements

With special thanks to the many helpful vegetable farmers at the Virginia SA Expo 1996.

The author and publishers are grateful to the following for permission to reproduce copyright material:

Cover: Coo-ee Picture Library

Australian Picture Library, pp. 16 © J. Carnemolla, 17 © Gerry Whitmont, 21; Coo-ee Picture Library, pp. 6, 8, 11, 12, 15, 22, 25, 26, 27, 29; Great Southern Stock, pp. 5, 13, 30; John McCammon/OSF, p. 24; NATFOTO/ANT Photo Library, p. 20; Otto Rogge/ANT Photo Library, p. 19; Stock Photos/Owen Hughes, p. 4; Dennis Sarson/LOCHMAN Transparencies, pp. 14, 23; Len Stewart/LOCHMAN Transparencies, p. 9; Harold Taylor/OSF, p. 18; Cyril Webster/ANT Photo Library, pp. 7, 10, 28.

First published 1998 by
MACMILLAN EDUCATION AUSTRALIA PTY LTD
627 Chapel Street, South Yarra 3141
10 9 8 7 6 5 4 3
08 07 06 05 04 03 02 01 00

Associated companies and representatives throughout the world

National Library of Australia cataloguing in publication data

Thomas, Ann
Vegetable farms.

Includes index.
ISBN 0 7329 4375 2.

1. Vegetables – Juvenile literature. 2. Farms – Juvenile literature. I. Title. (Series : Farms).

635

Text design by Polar Design
Cover design by Linda Forss
Typeset in Officinaprim by Alena Jencik of Grand Graphix Pty Ltd
Printed in Hong Kong

Contents

What is a farm?

Land can be used to grow crops or raise animals. This land is called a farm.

People who work on farms are called farmers.
There are many different types of farm.

Vegetable farms

Farms where vegetables are grown are called vegetable farms. Most farmers grow several different vegetable crops each year.

Most vegetable plants produce vegetables for only one year. New seeds or seedlings must be planted the next year.

Types of vegetable

There are many different types of vegetable. Some vegetables are called root vegetables. This is because we eat their roots. Potatoes, beetroot, turnips, carrots, radishes, garlic and ginger are all root vegetables.

Some vegetables are called leafy vegetables. This is because we eat their leaves. Spinach and silverbeet are both leafy vegetables.

Many vegetables grow on plants. Zucchini, eggplant, capsicum, peas, beans, corn, pumpkin, Brussels sprouts and broccoli all grow on plants.

Other vegetables are the whole plant. Leeks, onions, asparagus, mushrooms, cauliflower, lettuce and cabbage are examples of this type of vegetable.

Cultivation

Before a crop is planted, the farmer prepares the soil. A tractor pulls a cultivator to plough the paddock. It turns the soil over and digs grasses and **weeds** into the soil.

The soil is tested to see if a special type of plant food, called **fertiliser**, is needed. Fertiliser is added before seeds or seedlings are planted.

Each vegetable needs special soil, fertiliser, water and temperature conditions to grow. If there is not enough water, or the soil is poor, or it is too hot or cold, the plants will not grow well.

If there is too much rain, or the soil is too rich, the plants may rot, or grow too leafy. Once the plants are in the soil, farmers work hard to keep the conditions nearly perfect.

Caring for the crop

Young plants are checked regularly for disease and pests. Side shoots must be removed on some bushy plants like capsicum and corn.

Thinning makes the plant stronger and helps it to grow fewer, but larger, vegetables.

How vegetables grow

Each vegetable grows in a different way. Some plants, such as beans, grow best when the plants climb up a **stake.** This helps the plant to grow tall and produce many vegetables.

Zucchini, pumpkins, artichokes and eggplant all need large areas on the ground to grow. Farmers need to have space around these plants, so that they can easily weed, spray, water and pick the ripe vegetables.

Celery, asparagus and potatoes are grown in **trenches**. The trenches are then mounded as the plant begins to grow. Mounding is pushing more soil or compost around the roots and base of the plant. It protects the roots and keeps the plant firmly in the ground.

Other vegetables like onions, leeks and beetroot grow half in and half out of the soil. The whole plant gets pulled out at harvest and the farmers sell the **bulb** as food.

Watering and mulching

Almost all vegetables need to be watered as they grow. Farmers cannot always rely on regular rainfall.

Mulch is placed on the soil around the plants to keep the roots cool, to help stop weeds from growing and to keep the soil moist.

Diseases

Vegetable crops need to be sprayed with a special liquid to stop **fungi**, **bacteria** and **viruses** from attacking them.

Farmers also need to spray to keep pests away from the crops. Snails, slugs, aphids, millipedes, grubs, earwigs and cutworms are all pests. Larger animals like rabbits, birds, dogs and cats can also damage crops, but are harder to control.

Harvest

At **harvest** time most vegetables are picked by hand. Hand harvesting keeps the softer vegetables from being bruised or squashed.

Potatoes and other root vegetables are usually harvested by machine. The machine digs deep and turns the soil, then people collect the vegetables.

Packing and marketing

Vegetables are cleaned on the farm. They are sorted, tied in bunches or packed in boxes and trays before being sent to market.

Many farmers take their crops to central markets where they are sold to shopkeepers and restaurants. Some farmers sell their extra vegetables to local shops or at roadside stands.

After harvest, the farmers prepare their land for the next season's crop. **Compost** is dug into the soil before new crops are planted. Different crops are grown in different paddocks each year, to help keep the soil healthy.

Glossary

bacteria very tiny living things which sometimes cause disease

bulb an underground stem, with leaves above and roots below

compost fertiliser made from rotting vegetables and grasses

fertiliser rich nutrients added to the soil to improve it

fungi plants without leaves or flowers which sometimes grow on other plants

harvest the time to pick and gather vegetables

mulch a mixture of grass, leaves or straw placed on the ground to stop weeds from growing and to keep the soil damp

stake a thick pointed stick pushed into the ground for plants to grow up

trenches long dug out areas in the ground

viruses very tiny plants or animals that cause disease

weeds plants that grow where they are not wanted

Index